LEARN TO READ

PHONICS

Stories and Activities

R-CONTROLLED VOWELS, VOWEL TEAMS, DIPHTHONGS

Valerie Petrillo

© Valerie Petrillo 2024 All Rights Reserved

ISBN: 9798336932386

LEARN TO READ

PHONICS

Stories and Activities

This book belongs to:

_____

Name

© Valerie Petrillo 2024 All Rights Reserved

Parent Guide to Phonics

Children should learn phonics in an organized, structured way. A typical *scope and sequence* for kindergarten and first grade follows. Scope refers to *what* will be taught. Sequence is *the order* in which it will be taught.

1. **Short vowel consonant words** such as: *sat* and *cup*.

2. **Blends:** A blend is two consonants in a row. Each consonant says its own name. An example is *sp* in *spot*. There are many blends. Some examples are: cr, bl, st, pr, ld, nd and fr.

3. **Digraphs:** ff, ll, ss, zz, ck, sh, th, ch, ng, and nk. A digraph is two letters in a row that make one sound. An example for each of these would be: *cuff, mess, fuzz, tack, ship, this, chip, ring* and *sink*.

4. **Long vowel words with silent e** at the end. Examples would be: *cake (a), bike (i), rope (o), mute (u), and theme (e)*.

5. **Soft c and soft g:** An example of a soft c word is: *rice*. An example of a soft g word is: *gem*.

6. **Common endings:** es (for words ending in s, ch, ch, sh, ss, x, or z) ed, ing, y (long i) y (long e), le. An example for each of these would be: *dresses, camped, singing, fly, sandy, handle.*

7. **R-Controlled vowels:** Words where the r changes the sound of the vowel. Examples are: *car, fern, dirt, corn* and *fur.*

8. **Common vowel teams:** Two or more vowels in a row that make one sound. ai, ay, ee, ea, ie, igh, ou, ow, oa. An example for each of these would be: *paid, say, feed, bead, pie, night, pout, cow,* and *coat.*

9. **Diphthongs:** A diphthong is when two vowels make two sounds as they glide together. For example *oi* in *oil, oy* in *toy, ou* in *tour, ow* in *cow, oo* in *book.*

10. **Simple multisyllabic words:** Compound words such as: cup + cake = *cupcake.* Words with simple prefixes and suffixes such as: thank + ful = *thankful* and un + pack = *unpack.*

11. **Complex multisyllabic words:** Words with advanced prefixes and suffixes and three or more syllables.

Workbook Pages

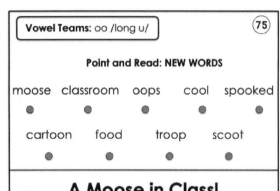

THE STORY

You: Read the new words and the story.

Together: Read the new words and the story.

Child: Reads the new words and the story.

BLEND THE SOUNDS

You: Show your child how to blend the sounds together. For example the word *pool*: /p/ +/long u/ + /l/

Together: Blend the sounds WITH your child.

Child: Blends the sounds independently.

Child: Draws a line from the word to the matching picture.

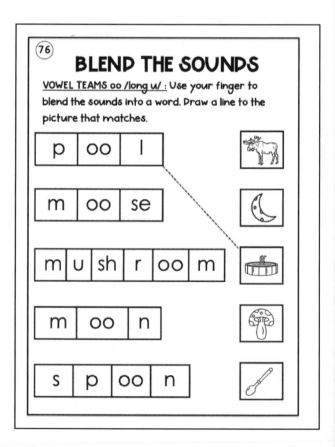

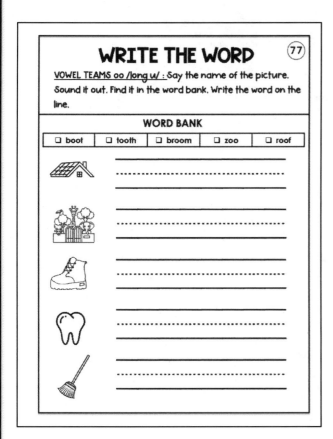

WRITE THE WORD

You: Point and say the names of all the pictures. Show your child how to build the word. For example:

The sounds I hear are:
/r/ + /long u/ + /f/

What word says these sounds in the word bank?
roof... it has letter r for /r/, the vowel team oo for /long u/ and letter f for /f/.

Together: Repeat the word building.

Child: Builds the word independently and writes it on the line. Puts a check in the box.

WORD SORT

You: Point and say the name of the two word sort categories. For example: **oo** words and **ey** words. Read the words in the boxes. Ask, *where does tool go? Where does key go?*

Together: Repeat the word sorting.

Child: Blends the sounds independently.

Child: Reads each word in the word box, writes it under **oo** or **ey** and checks the box.

Table of Contents

SOFT C and SOFT G

1. soft c /s/: *Mice on the Ice* p. 11
2. soft g /j/: *A Strange Bird* p. 15

COMMON ENDINGS

3. es: *Lunch on Benches* p.19
4. ed: *A Fun Day* p. 23
5. ing: *Looking For Whales* p. 27

TRIGRAPHS

6. tch /ch/: *Mitch will Pitch* p. 31
7. dge /j/: *Madge and Gus* p. 35

R-CONTROLLED VOWELS

8. ar /ar/: *The Farm* p. 39
9. or, ore /or/: *Corn on the Cob* p. 43
10. er /er/: *Mister Frosty* p. 47
11. ir, ur /er/: *Time for School* p. 51

COMMON VOWEL TEAMS

12. ai, ay /long a/: *Birthday Surprise p. 55*
13. ee, ea, ey /long e/: *A Turkey Feast p. 59*
14. oa, ow, oe /long o/: *Along the Coast p. 63*
15. e, igh /long i/ : *Lightning p. 67*
16. oo, u /oo/ (as in book): *The Big, Big Fish p. 71*
17. oo /long u/: *A Moose in Class! P. 75*
18. ew, ui, ue /long u/: *Newborn Birds p. 79*
19. au, aw, augh /aw/: *The Hawk p. 83*
20. ea /short a/, a /short o/: *A Rainy Breakfast p. 87*

DIPHTHONGS

21. oi, oy /oi/: *Garden Joy p. 91*
22. ou, ow /ow/: *Bounce House p. 95*

ANSWER KEY *p. 99*

Soft c: ce /s/

Point and Read: NEW WORDS

mice   ice   race   pace   dance

nice   place   grace   lace

Mice on Ice

I saw mice at the ice rink! The mice had a race. They went at a fast pace! Next some dogs did a dance. It was a nice dance. Then a skunk got on the ice! He had a black and white face. The skunk stunk up the place! Last I saw a duck skate by with grace. She had a lace cape. This ice rink is a funny place!

… 12

BLEND THE SOUNDS

<u>SOFT c:</u> Use your finger to blend the sounds into a word. Draw a line to the picture that matches.

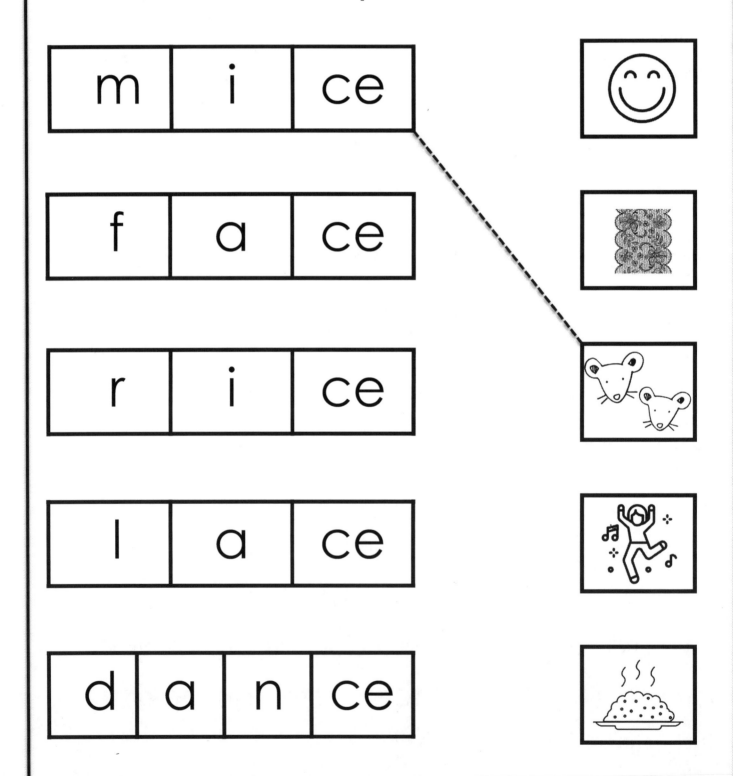

WRITE THE WORD

⑬

SOFT c: Say the name of the picture. Sound it out. Find it in the word bank. Write the word on the line.

WORD BANK

| ❑ race | ❑ dice | ❑ ice | ❑ space | ❑ fence |

_____

_____

_____

_____

Word Sort
Soft c and long o

14

- ☐ spice ☐ bone ☐ mice ☐ drone ☐ fence
- ☐ tone   ☐ grace ☐ lone ☐ nice ☐ spoke

Write the soft c words here:

Write the long o words here:

Soft g: ge /j/

Point and Read: NEW WORDS

strange　　huge　　range　　plunge　　page

change

A Strange Bird

I went to the pond with my bird book. I saw a strange bird in the sky! It had huge wings. The range of its wings was wide! The bird took a plunge in the pond. The bird was not on any page in my book. Next, the bird made a change. It flew up, up, up to the sky. The strange bird flew away. The bird with the huge wings was fun to see.

BLEND THE SOUNDS

<u>SOFT g</u>: Use your finger to blend the sounds into a word. Draw a line to the picture that matches.

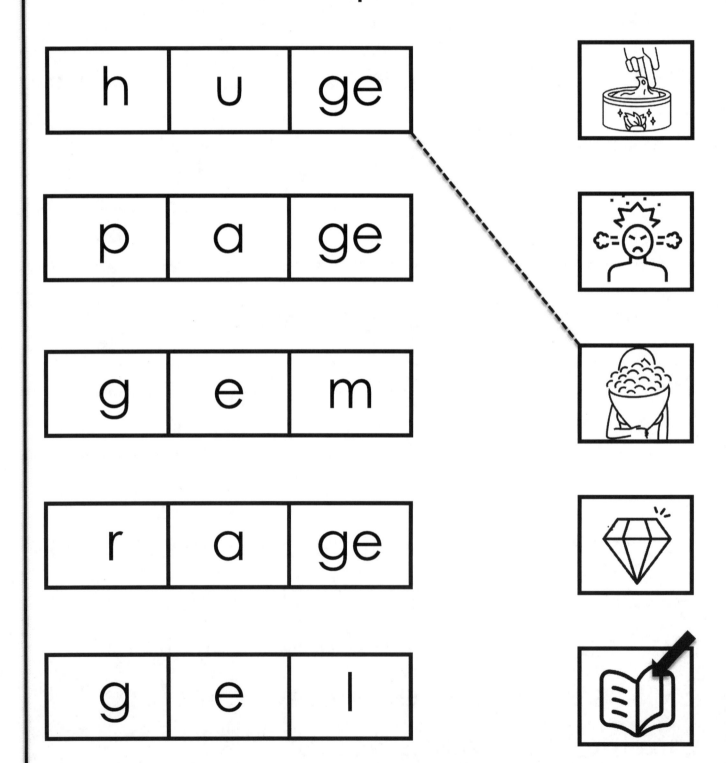

WRITE THE WORD

17

SOFT g: Say the name of the picture. Sound it out. Find it in the word bank. Write the word on the line.

WORD BANK

| ❏ rage | ❏ huge | ❏ gem | ❏ cage | ❏ page |

Word Sort
Soft g and soft c

☐ sage ☐ lace ☐ gem ☐ face ☐ cage
☐ nice ☐ gel ☐ dice ☐ rage ☐ mice

Write the <u>soft g</u> words here:

Write the <u>soft c</u> words here:

Ending: es

Point and Read: NEW WORDS

lunches   benches   glasses   dishes   boxes

buzzes   classes   buses

Lunch on Benches

Today is hot! We will eat our lunches on benches. Seth will bring the glasses. I will bring the dishes. Rick will bring boxes of napkins. Time for lunch! A fly buzzes by as we eat. When lunch is over we go back to classes. We have math class and music. Soon it is time to line up. We take the buses home.

(20) # BLEND THE SOUNDS

ENDING es: Use your finger to blend the sounds into a word. Draw a line to the picture that matches.

| l | u | n | ch | e | s |

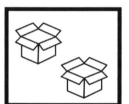

| b | o | x | e | s |

| d | i | sh | e | s |

| b | u | s | e | s |

| d | r | e | ss | e | s |

WRITE THE WORD

ENDING es: Say the name of the picture. Sound it out. Find it in the word bank. Write the word on the line.

WORD BANK

❑ kisses ❑ brushes ❑ foxes ❑ benches ❑ glasses

Word Sort

(22) — Endings es and s

- ❏ foxes ❏ cats ❏ buses ❏ tops ❏ dishes
- ❏ hats ❏ boxes ❏ fins ❏ kisses ❏ huts

Write the es words here:

Write the ending s words here:

Ending: ed

Point and Read: NEW WORDS

pumped   picked   mixed   frosted   called

blasted   rocked   chomped   thanked   rested

were

A Fun Day

Liz and Tess were pumped for a fun day. Liz picked roses and put them in a vase. Tess mixed up a cake and frosted it. They called Jack, Ron, and Kat to come over. Liz blasted the tunes. They rocked to a new dance. Then it was time for cake. Yum! They chomped it down! Jack, Ron, and Kat thanked them. They went home and Liz and Tess rested!

BLEND THE SOUNDS

ENDING ed: Use your finger to blend the sounds into a word. Draw a line to the picture that matches.

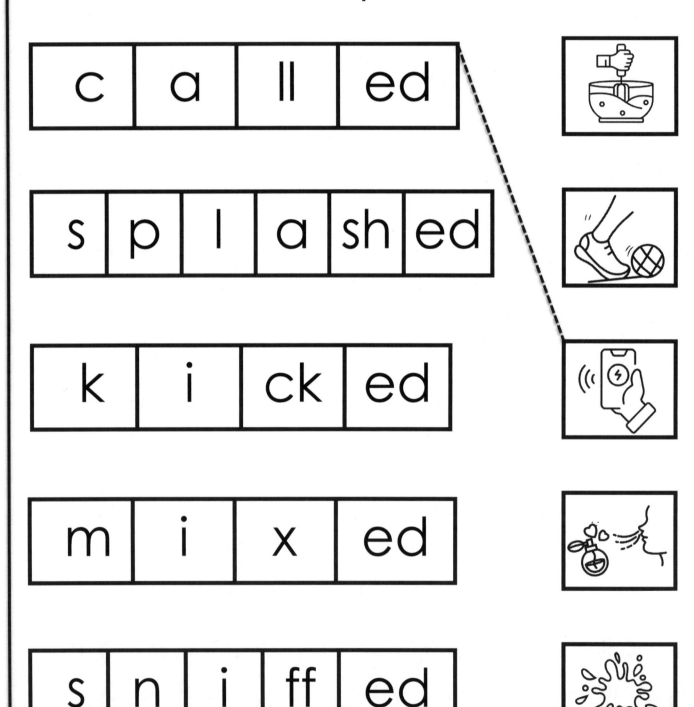

WRITE THE WORD

(25)

ENDING ed: Say the name of the picture. Sound it out. Find it in the word bank. Write the word on the line.

WORD BANK

| ❏ picked | ❏ melted | ❏ locked | ❏ spilled | ❏ jumped |

Word Sort

(26)

Ending: ed
Blend: st

- ☐ kicked
- ☐ stop
- ☐ sniffed
- ☐ still
- ☐ picked
- ☐ stick
- ☐ spilled
- ☐ stand
- ☐ filled
- ☐ step

Write the ed words here:

Write the st words here:

Ending: ing

Point and Read: NEW WORDS

looking   crashing   going

splashing   hanging   winking

Looking for Whales

Ben and Tim were on a ship. They were looking for whales. Then… a big whale came crashing by! The whale was going up and down in the waves. It was splashing the ship. Ben and Tim were hanging onto the sides. They did not want to fall off the ship! Then the big whale left. It looked like it was winking when it swam away!

BLEND THE SOUNDS

ENDING ing: Use your finger to blend the sounds into a word. Draw a line to the picture that matches.

| b | r | u | sh | i | ng |

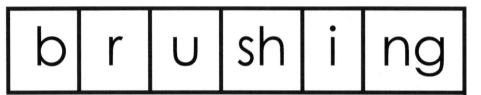

| d | r | i | nk | i | ng |

| s | i | ng | i | ng |

| d | u | s | t | i | ng |

| f | i | sh | i | ng |

WRITE THE WORD

(29)

ENDING ing: Say the name of the picture. Sound it out. Find it in the word bank. Write the word on the line.

WORD BANK

| ❑ winking | ❑ hanging | ❑ planting | ❑ helping | ❑ rocking |

Word Sort

(30)

Ending: ing
Blend: gr

- ☐ packing
- ☐ grass
- ☐ ringing
- ☐ sinking
- ☐ grin
- ☐ banking
- ☐ grape
- ☐ grip
- ☐ pushing
- ☐ grill

Write the ing words here:

Write the gr words here:

Trigraph: tch /ch/

Point and Read: NEW WORDS

Mitch   pitch   patch   match   catch

Mitch will Pitch

Mitch is going to pitch at his baseball game. But Mitch also has a problem. He has a hole in his pants! Mitch has to patch up the hole. He got a red patch to match his red pants. Now his pants are fixed. Next he has to catch a bus to the game. He rode the bus until it came to a stop. Then, Mitch jumped off the bus. It was time for Mitch to pitch!

BLEND THE SOUNDS

TRIGRAPH tch: Use your finger to blend the sounds into a word. Draw a line to the picture that matches.

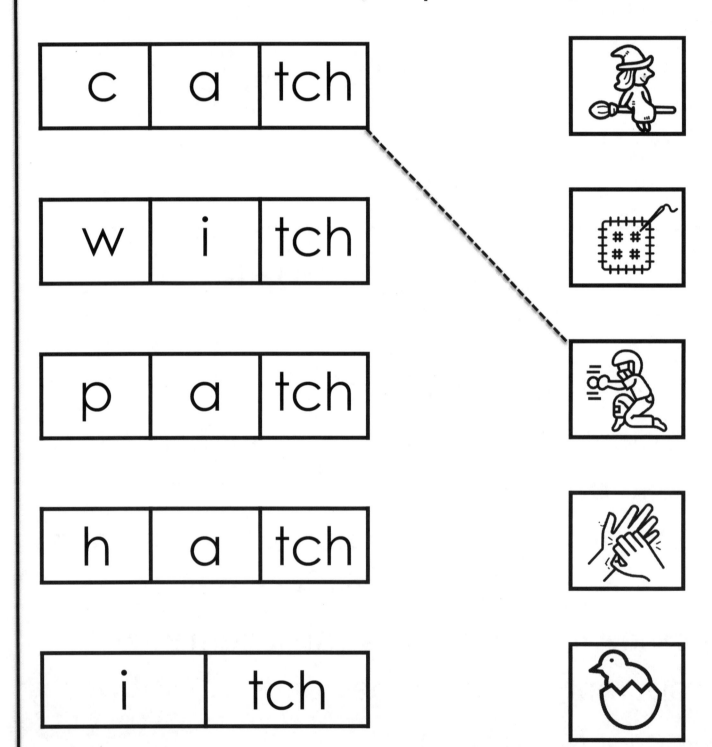

WRITE THE WORD

(33)

TRIGRAPH tch: Say the name of the picture. Sound it out. Find it in the word bank. Write the word on the line.

WORD BANK

| ☐ crutch | ☐ hatch | ☐ pitch | ☐ match | ☐ latch |

Word Sort

Trigraph: tch
Digraph: sh

(34)

☐ patch ☐ shell ☐ ditch ☐ shack ☐ clutch
☐ shape ☐ hitch ☐ shop ☐ witch ☐ shut

Write the tch words here:

Write the sh words here:

Trigraph: dge /j/

Point and Read: NEW WORDS

Madge   bridge   edge   lodge   hedge

budge   fridge

Madge and Gus

Madge and Gus made a town with blocks. Gus made a long bridge for the town. Madge made a pond with blue blocks. The pond was at the edge of the town. Gus made a small lodge. He made a green hedge in front of the lodge. It was time for lunch. Madge and Gus did not want to budge. So, Madge put their lunch in the fridge!

BLEND THE SOUNDS

TRIGRAPH dge: Use your finger to blend the sounds into a word. Draw a line to the picture that matches.

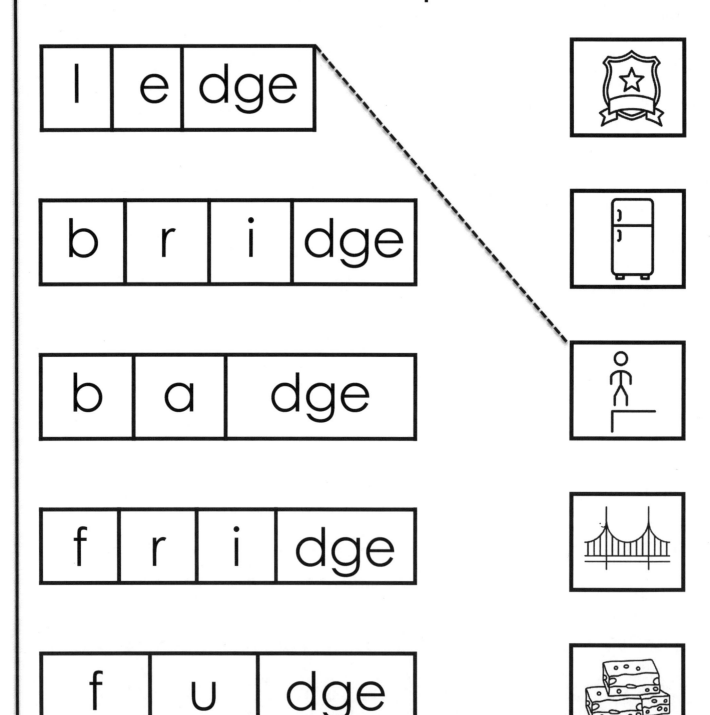

WRITE THE WORD

(37)

TRIGRAPH dge: Say the name of the picture. Sound it out. Find it in the word bank. Write the word on the line.

WORD BANK

| ❏ wedge | ❏ pledge | ❏ lodge | ❏ judge | ❏ bridge |

1. judge
2. lodge
3. bridge
4. pledge
5. wedge

Word Sort

Trigraph: dge
Digraph: ck

(38)

☐ duck ☐ fudge ☐ lick ☐ edge ☐ tack
☐ ledge ☐ sick ☐ judge ☐ pick ☐ lodge

Write the <u>dge</u> words here:

Write the <u>ck</u> words here:

R Controlled Vowels: ar /ar/

Point and Read: NEW WORDS

Clark   farm   farmland   large   garden

charge   Shar   Lark   barnyard   hard   part

The Farm

Clark Farm is very big. It has lots of farmland. The farm has a large garden and a barn. Mark works hard at Clark Farm. He is in charge of the pigs and chickens. Mark also plants and tends to the crops. Shar and Lark are cats that live in the barnyard. The cats work hard to keep the mice away. Shar and Lark are part of Clark Farm too!

BLEND THE SOUNDS

<u>ar words:</u> Use your finger to blend the sounds into a word. Draw a line to the picture that matches.

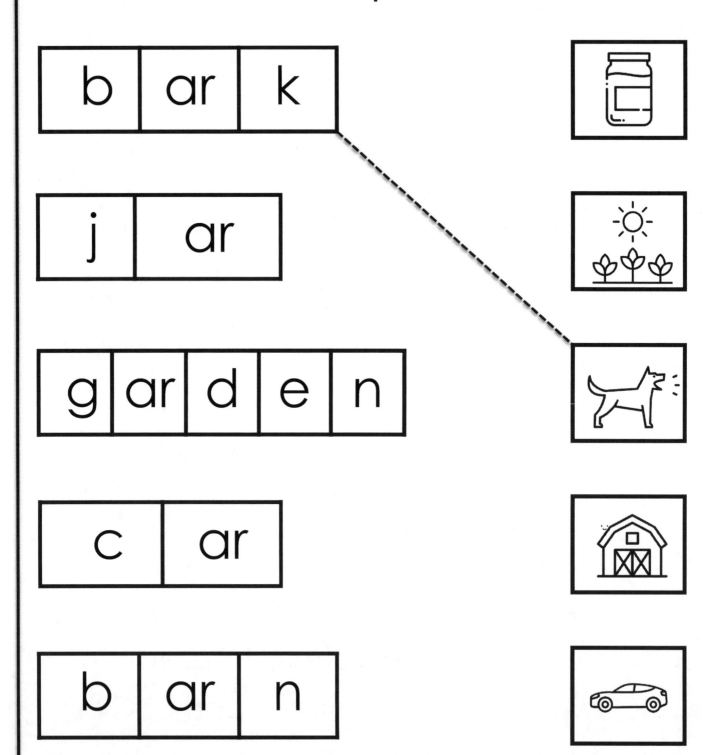

WRITE THE WORD

41

ar words: Say the name of the picture. Sound it out. Find it in the word bank. Write the word on the line.

WORD BANK

| ☐ shark | ☐ scarf | ☐ yarn | ☐ star | ☐ dart |

Word Sort

42

R-vowels: ar
Blend: br

- ☐ tar
- ☐ brick
- ☐ cart
- ☐ bride
- ☐ part
- ☐ brim
- ☐ march
- ☐ brisk
- ☐ start
- ☐ brush

Write the ar words here:

Write the br words here:

R Controlled Vowels: or /or/

Point and Read: NEW WORDS

morning   Dorn   explored   corn   sort

transported   porch   chore   more

Corn on the Cob

This morning we went to the Farmers Market. Dorn and I explored the store. Then we got lots of corn on the cob! I love corn on the cob. We had to sort the corn into bags. Then Dorn and I transported the corn to the porch. It was our chore to take off the husks. Then Pop put them in a hot pot. Yum! It was time to eat the corn! I ate two and asked for more!

BLEND THE SOUNDS

<u>or /or/ words:</u> Use your finger to blend the sounds into a word. Draw a line to the picture that matches.

| p | o | p | c | or | n |

| c | or | n |

| f | or | k |

| h | or | n |

| s | t | ore |

WRITE THE WORD

(45)

or/or/ words: Say the name of the picture. Sound it out. Find it in the word bank. Write the word on the line.

WORD BANK

| ❏ forest | ❏ shorts | ❏ horse | ❏ storm | ❏ core |

Word Sort

46

R-vowels: or
Blend: fr

☐ tore   ☐ fresh   ☐ pork   ☐ frost   ☐ storm
☐ frill ☐ born   ☐ fret   ☐ sort   ☐ frame

Write the or words here:

Write the fr words here:

R Controlled Vowels: er/er/ (47)

Point and Read: NEW WORDS

Vern   winter   sister   Fern   under

her   over   mister   number

Mister Frosty

Vern saw snow falling. He ran out into the winter flakes. Next, his sister Fern ran out. Vern and Fern made a snow bridge and sat under it. Next they made a snowman. Fern put her hat on his head. Vern put a scarf over his neck. "I want to name him, Mister Frosty," said Fern. "OK," said Vern. "Mister Frosty is our number one snowman!"

BLEND THE SOUNDS

er /er/ words: Use your finger to blend the sounds into a word. Draw a line to the picture that matches.

| u | n | d | er |

| f | ar | m | er |

| l | e | tt | er |

| s | p | i | d | er |

| p | a | p | er |

WRITE THE WORD

(49)

er /er/ words: Say the name of the picture. Sound it out. Find it in the word bank. Write the word on the line.

WORD BANK

| ❑ boxer | ❑ camper | ❑ river | ❑ barber | ❑ tiger |

Word Sort

(50)

R-vowels: er
Digraph: th

☐ sister ☐ bath ☐ farmer ☐ this ☐ hunter
☐ sloth ☐ winter ☐ thin ☐ boxer ☐ thick

Write the er words here:

Write the th words here:

R Controlled Vowels: ir, ur /er/

Point and Read: NEW WORDS

first   third   shirt   skirt   curb

twirl   dirt   bird   chirps

Time for School

First I woke up. The second thing I did was to eat a pancake. Third, I put on my shirt and skirt. Time for school! I ran to the curb to catch the bus. The bus is not here. It is late! I twirl my hair while I wait. I dig in the dirt with a stick. A bird flies by and chirps, "Good Morning!" At last I see my bus! It is time for school."

BLEND THE SOUNDS

<u>ir, ur /er/ words:</u> Use your finger to blend the sounds into a word. Draw a line to the picture that matches.

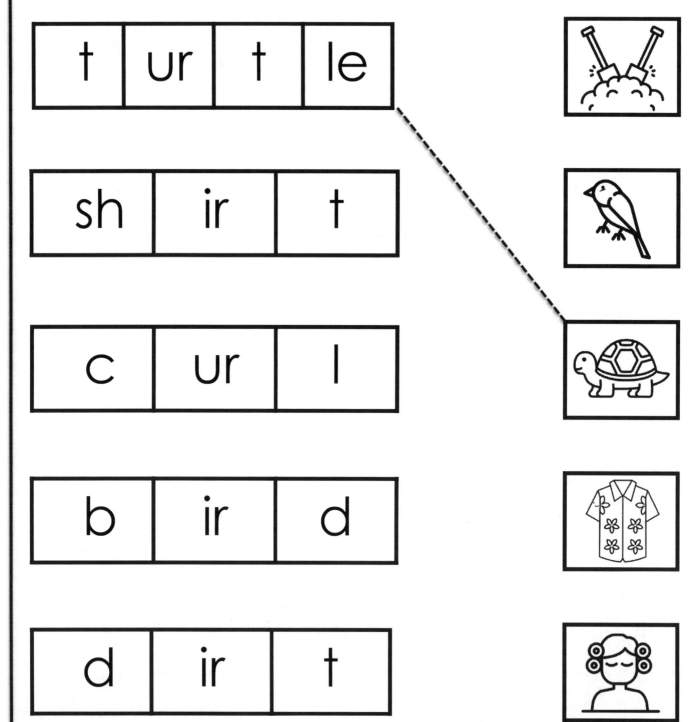

WRITE THE WORD

(53)

ir, ur /er/ words: Say the name of the picture. Sound it out. Find it in the word bank. Write the word on the line.

WORD BANK

| ❏ skirt | ❏ third | ❏ purse | ❏ surf | ❏ church |

54 Word Sort

R-vowels: ir
R-vowels: ur

- ☐ skirt
- ☐ dirt
- ☐ chirp
- ☐ girl
- ☐ stir
- ☐ nurse
- ☐ hurt
- ☐ blurt
- ☐ slurp
- ☐ hurl

Write the ir words here:

Write the ur words here:

Long Vowel Teams
ai, ay /long a/

Point and Read: NEW WORDS

| May | birthday | Friday | wait | Kay |
| train | tray | way | play | waiting |

Birthday Surprise

May has a birthday on Friday! She cannot wait! Kay will take May to the park. They will ride there on a train. May and Kay will have lunch on a tray. They will see lots of things on their way. When they get to the park they will get off to play. May has a fun surprise for Kay. May's friends will be waiting for her at the park! It will be a fun birthday.

BLEND THE SOUNDS

<u>VOWEL TEAMS ai, ay /long a/:</u> Use your finger to blend the sounds into a word. Draw a line to the picture that matches.

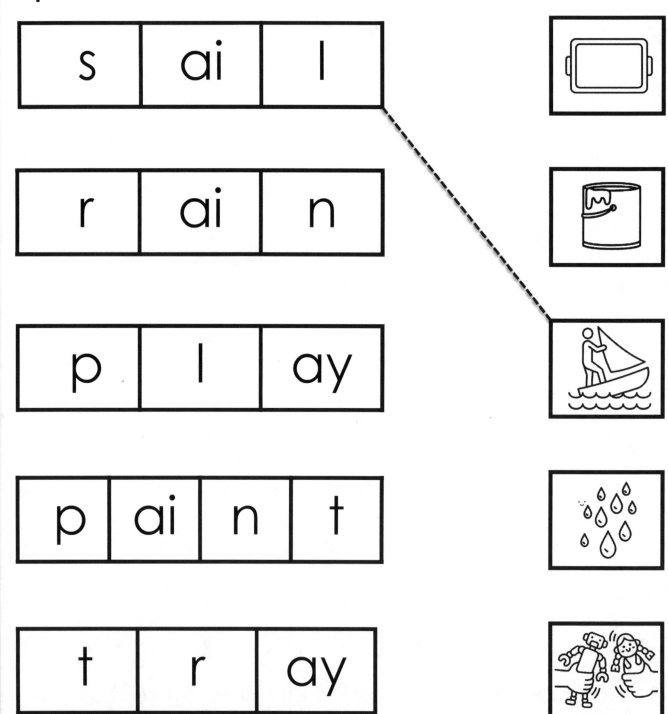

WRITE THE WORD

(57)

VOWEL TEAMS ai, ay /long a/: Say the name of the picture. Sound it out. Find it in the word bank. Write the word on the line.

WORD BANK

| ☐ hay | ☐ train | ☐ spray | ☐ snail | ☐ chain |

Word Sort

58

Vowel Team: ai
Vowel Team: ay

- ☐ gain
- ☐ gray
- ☐ main
- ☐ stay
- ☐ grain
- ☐ say
- ☐ paint
- ☐ lay
- ☐ chain
- ☐ pay

Write the ai words here:

Write the ay words here:

Long Vowel Teams: ee, ea, ey /long e/

Point and Read: NEW WORDS

turkey   heap   meat   green   beans

peach   plead   wheat   sweets   cream

reach   cheesecake   feast   beat

A Turkey Feast

We had a great turkey dinner! I put a heap of meat on my plate. Then I gobbled down green beans and gravy. My dog Peach sat under the table so that he could plead for scraps. I gave him a little wheat roll. After that, it was time for sweets! Baby sister had ice cream. I reached for the cheesecake. I love turkey dinner! It is a feast that cannot be beat!

BLEND THE SOUNDS

VOWEL TEAMS ee, ea, ey /long e/: Use your finger to blend the sounds into a word. Draw a line to the picture that matches.

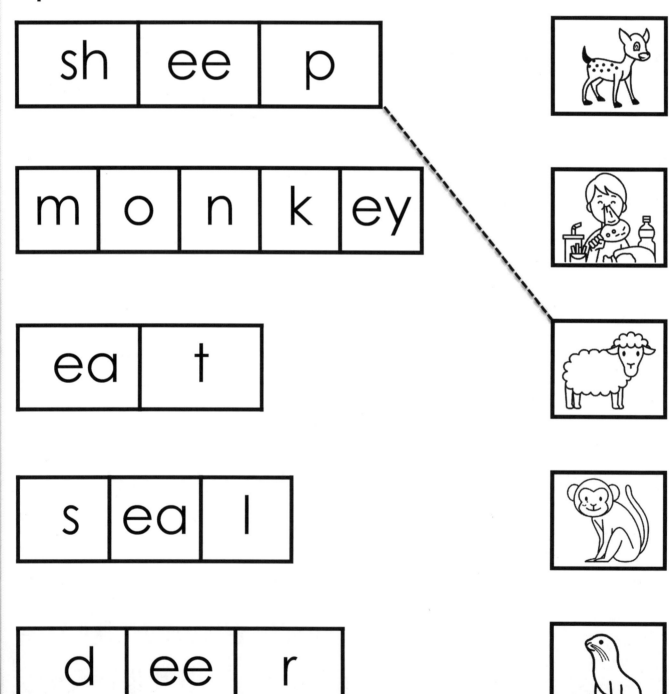

WRITE THE WORD

61

VOWEL TEAMS ee, ea, ey /long e/: Say the name of the picture. Sound it out. Find it in the word bank. Write the word on the line.

WORD BANK

| ☐ beach | ☐ key | ☐ tree | ☐ chimney | ☐ feet |

Word Sort

Vowel Team: ee
Vowel Team: ea

- ☐ seed ☐ steal ☐ deep ☐ steep ☐ cheat
- ☐ bead ☐ peel ☐ meal ☐ beat ☐ seek

Write the ee words here:

Write the ea words here:

Long Vowel Teams: oa, ow, oe /long o/

Point and Read: NEW WORDS

Joe　　Moe　　steamboat　　floated　　coast

glow　　rainbow　　show　　roadside　　boat

coastline

Along the Coast

Joe and Moe hopped on a steamboat. The steamboat floated along the coast and into the harbor. Joe and Moe saw the harbor glow with a rainbow. The rainbow put on quite a show! The boys explored the harbor. They got some roadside fish and fries. Joe and Moe got back on the boat. It was time to return to the coastline.

BLEND THE SOUNDS

VOWEL TEAMS oa, ow, oe /long o/: Use your finger to blend the sounds into a word. Draw a line to the picture that matches.

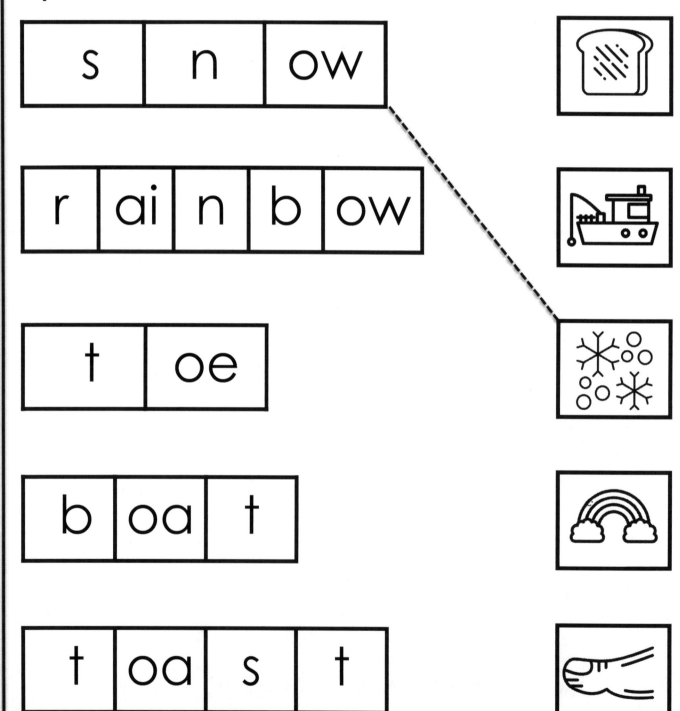

WRITE THE WORD

VOWEL TEAMS oa, ow, oe /long o/ : Say the name of the picture. Sound it out. Find it in the word bank. Write the word on the line.

WORD BANK

| ☐ soap | ☐ bow | ☐ blow | ☐ coat | ☐ Joe |

Word Sort

66

Vowel Team: oa
Vowel Team: ow

- ☐ soap
- ☐ bow
- ☐ goat
- ☐ grow
- ☐ toast
- ☐ tow
- ☐ float
- ☐ slow
- ☐ boat
- ☐ mow

Write the oa words here:

Write the ow words here:

Long Vowel Teams: ie, igh, /long i/

Point and Read: NEW WORDS

tonight   lightning   bright   nighttime   lights

sighting   right   delight   pie   fright

Lightning

Tonight I saw lightning. Have you ever seen how bright lightning can be? When it is nighttime, it lights up the whole sky! If there is a sighting of lightning, go inside. That is the right thing to do. It is safe inside. I think lightning is a delight to see. My dog, Pie does NOT like lightning. He thinks it is a fright to see!

BLEND THE SOUNDS

<u>VOWEL TEAMS ie, igh /long i/</u>: Use your finger to blend the sounds into a word. Draw a line to the picture that matches.

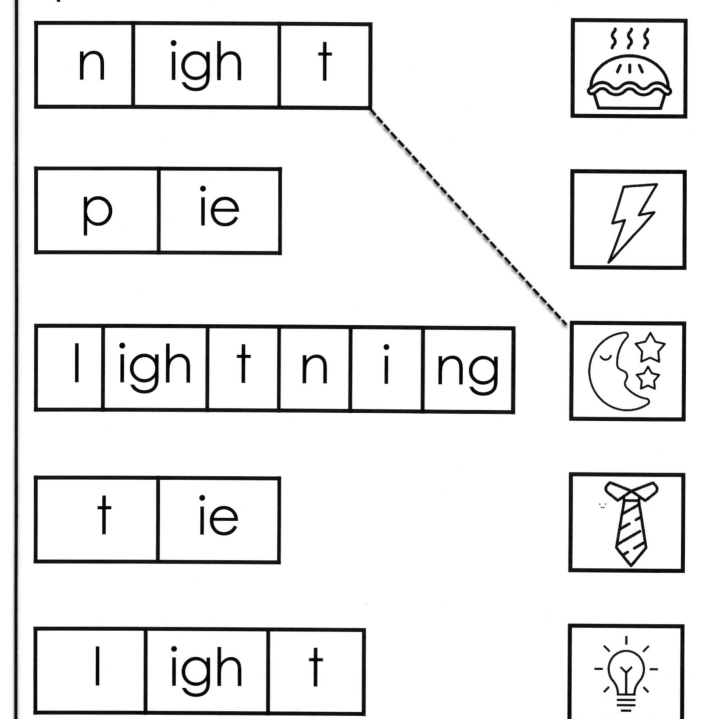

WRITE THE WORD

(69)

VOWEL TEAMS ie, igh /long i/ : Say the name of the picture. Sound it out. Find it in the word bank. Write the word on the line.

WORD BANK

| ☐ fight | ☐ flight | ☐ fries | ☐ die | ☐ cries |

Word Sort

70

Vowel Team: ie
Vowel Team: igh

- ☐ tie
- ☐ night
- ☐ pie
- ☐ might
- ☐ dried
- ☐ bright
- ☐ lie
- ☐ sight
- ☐ flies
- ☐ fight

Write the ie words here:

Write the igh words here:

Vowel Teams: oo, u /oo/ (as in book)

Point and Read: NEW WORDS

Brook   put   hook   pulled   good   took

cook   wood   looked   cooked   full

The Big, Big Fish

Brook and his dad went fishing. Brook put his hook into the pond and pulled up a big, big fish! "Good job, Brook," his dad said. His dad took at pic of Brook and the fish. Next, it was time to cook the fish. They both gathered wood for a fire. Brook looked on as dad lit the fire. Brook put the fish in a pan and cooked it. Dad and Brook ate the big, big fish. Soon Brook and his dad were full!

BLEND THE SOUNDS

(72)

<u>VOWEL TEAMS oo, u /oo/ as in book:</u> Use your finger to blend the sounds into a word. Draw a line to the picture that matches.

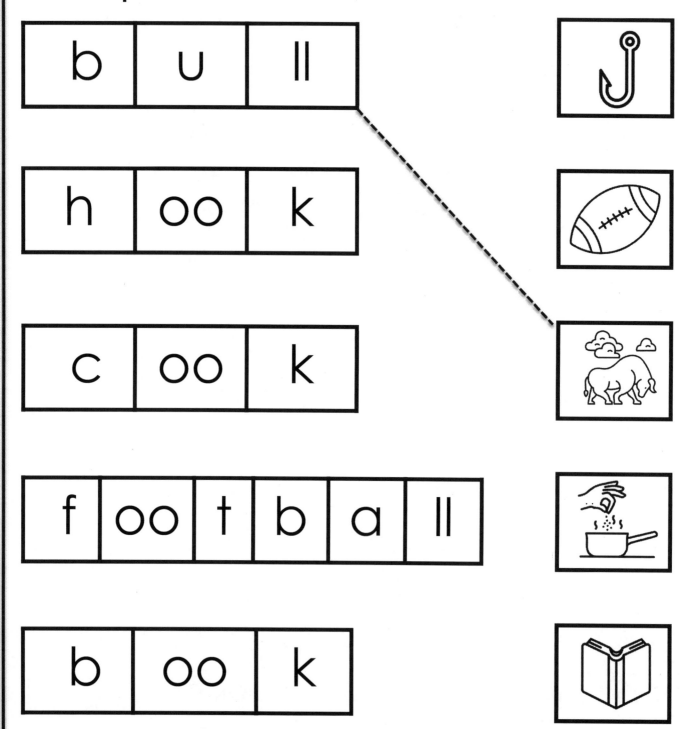

WRITE THE WORD

(73)

VOWEL TEAMS oo, u /oo/ as in book: Say the name of the picture. Sound it out. Find it in the word bank. Write the word on the line.

WORD BANK

| ☐ pull | ☐ foot | ☐ look | ☐ wood | ☐ cook |

Word Sort

(74)

Vowel Team: ull
Vowel Team: oo

☐ bull   ☐ book   ☐ pull   ☐ foot   ☐ pulls
☐ took   ☐ full   ☐ cook   ☐ bulls   ☐ hook

Write the ull words here:

Write the oo words here:

Vowel Teams: oo /long u/

(75)

Point and Read: NEW WORDS

moose   classroom   oops   cool   spooked

cartoon   food   troop   scoot

A Moose in Class!

I live in Alaska where there are lots of moose. One day a moose walked into the classroom! Oops! I was trying to act cool but some kids were spooked. It was like a cartoon! His head was up to the ceiling. I think the moose was looking for food. A troop of wildlife police came in to get the moose. It was time for the moose to scoot!

BLEND THE SOUNDS

<u>VOWEL TEAMS oo /long u/</u> : Use your finger to blend the sounds into a word. Draw a line to the picture that matches.

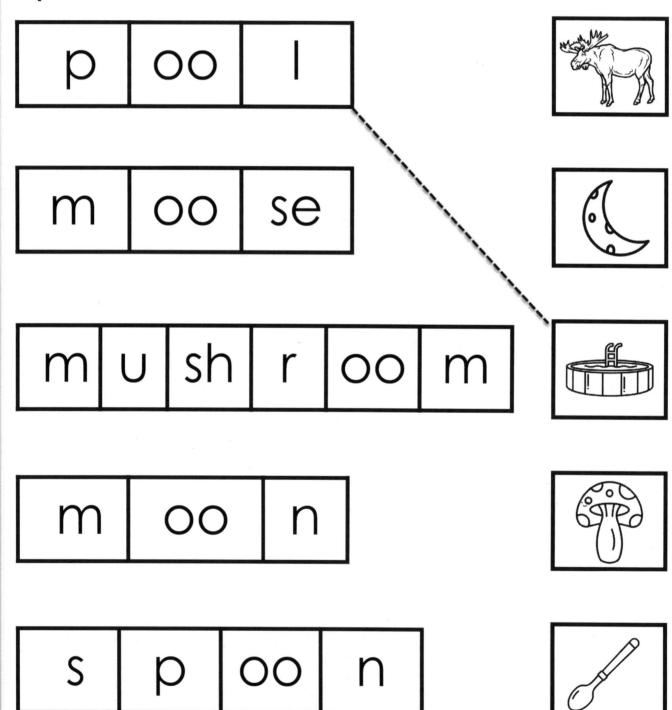

WRITE THE WORD

(77)

VOWEL TEAMS oo /long u/ : Say the name of the picture. Sound it out. Find it in the word bank. Write the word on the line.

WORD BANK

| ❏ boot | ❏ tooth | ❏ broom | ❏ zoo | ❏ roof |

78 # Word Sort

Vowel Team: oo
Vowel Team: ey

- ☐ tool
- ☐ turkey
- ☐ zoom
- ☐ alley
- ☐ fool
- ☐ key
- ☐ groom
- ☐ donkey
- ☐ moon
- ☐ keys

Write the oo words here:

Write the ey words here:

Vowel Teams: ew, ui, ue /long u/

Point and Read: NEW WORDS

Drew   Sue   suitcase   newborn   flew

fruit   chew   crew   drew

Newborn Birds

Drew and Sue found an old suitcase in the woods. In it was a nest with newborn baby birds! The bird mom flew down to the nest. She fed them tiny bits of fruit and worms. Drew and Sue watched the little birds chew up their food. The baby birds were a cute crew. The mom bird drew them close to her and they fell asleep.

BLEND THE SOUNDS

<u>VOWEL TEAMS ew, ui, ue /long u/</u>: Use your finger to blend the sounds into a word. Draw a line to the picture that matches.

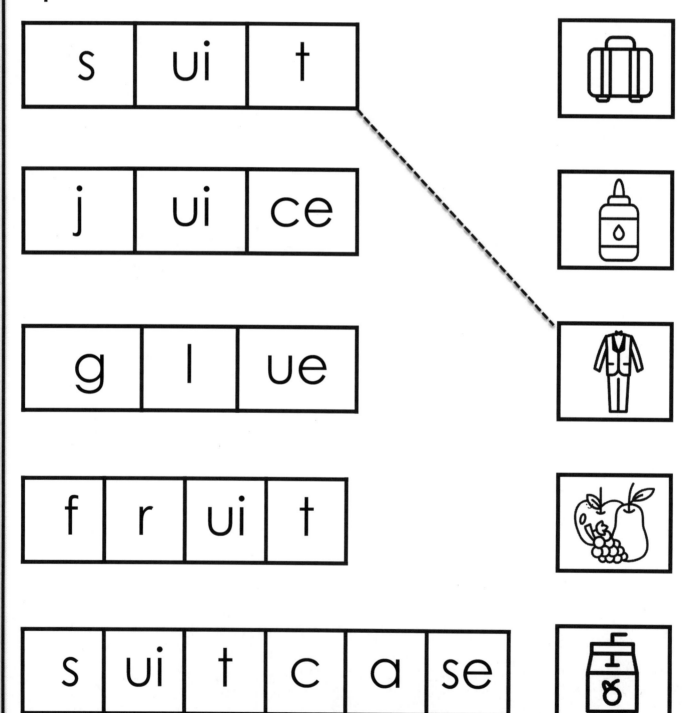

WRITE THE WORD

81

VOWEL TEAMS ew, ui, ue /long u/: Say the name of the picture. Sound it out. Find it in the word bank. Write the word on the line.

WORD BANK

| ❏ clue | ❏ blue | ❏ screw | ❏ flew | ❏ cruise |

Word Sort

82

Vowel Team: ui
Vowel Team: ue

- ☐ sue
- ☐ fruit
- ☐ blue
- ☐ bruise
- ☐ true
- ☐ juice
- ☐ due
- ☐ suit
- ☐ glue
- ☐ cruise

Write the ui words here:

Write the ue words here:

Vowel Teams: au, aw, augh /aw/

Point and Read: NEW WORDS

saw   hawk   launch   dawn   lawn

sprawl   Paul   pause   claws   squawk

The Hawk

At dawn, I saw a hawk launch into the sky. It passed over my lawn. I watched his wings sprawl ever so wide. He looked like a small plane! Even my dog Paul took a pause to look up. Then, the hawk landed on my fence with his claws. "Squawk!" The hawk said, "Squawk, squawk, squawk!" I put my hands over my ears. It was time for Paul and I to say good-bye to the hawk!

BLEND THE SOUNDS

<u>VOWEL TEAMS au, aw, augh /aw/</u>: Use your finger to blend the sounds into a word. Draw a line to the picture that matches.

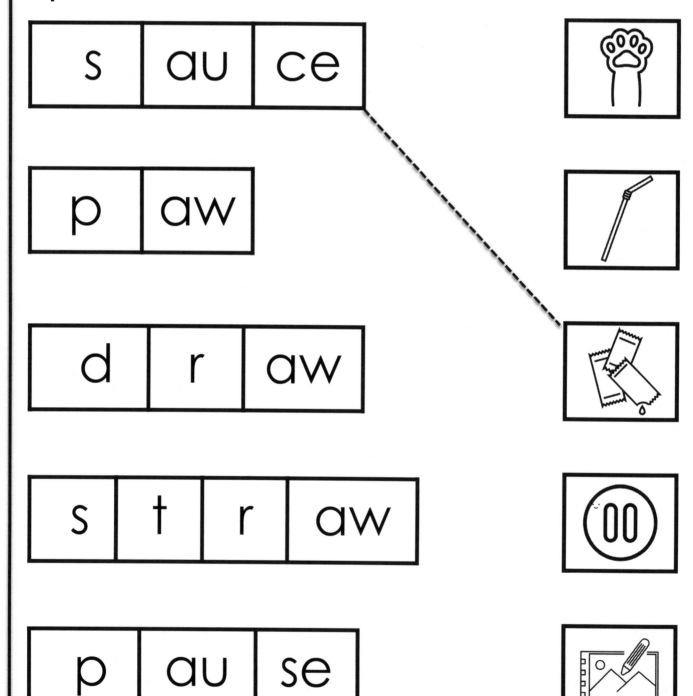

WRITE THE WORD

(85)

VOWEL TEAMS au, aw, augh /aw/: Say the name of the picture. Sound it out. Find it in the word bank. Write the word on the line.

WORD BANK

| ☐ caught | ☐ yawn | ☐ claw | ☐ August | ☐ fawn |

Word Sort

(86)

Vowel Team: au
Vowel Team: aw

- ☐ cause
- ☐ draw
- ☐ gauze
- ☐ lawn
- ☐ launch
- ☐ jaw
- ☐ pause
- ☐ flaw
- ☐ haul
- ☐ dawn

Write the au words here:

Write the aw words here:

Vowel Teams: ea /short e/   a /short o/

Point and Read: NEW WORDS

breakfast   want   waffles   Heather   father

spread   bread   heavy   water   steady

ready   swap

A Rainy Breakfast

Time for breakfast! "I want waffles!" Heather said to dad. Her father made waffles and bacon. Heather spread bread with jelly. A heavy jug of water and lemon sat on the table. Rain fell at a steady pace outside as they worked. Finally, they were ready to eat! "I will swap you a waffle for jelly bread," dad said. "Good deal!" said Heather.

BLEND THE SOUNDS

(88)

<u>VOWEL TEAMS ea /short e/ a /short o/</u>: Use your finger to blend the sounds into a word. Draw a line to the picture that matches.

| w | a | ff | le |

| b | r | ea | d |

| w | a | t | er |

| f | ea | th | er |

| w | a | tch |

WRITE THE WORD

(89)

VOWEL TEAMS ea /short e/ a /short o/ : Say the name of the picture. Sound it out. Find it in the word bank. Write the word on the line.

WORD BANK

| ❏ swan | ❏ wand | ❏ sweater | ❏ wash | ❏ head |

Word Sort

90

Vowel Team: ea
Vowel : a

☐ head ☐ watch ☐ bread ☐ swap ☐ tread
☐ wash ☐ spread ☐ swan ☐ sweat ☐ wand

Write the ea words here:

Write the a words here:

Diphthongs: oi, oy /oi/

Point and Read: NEW WORDS

Roy   Joy   enjoy   soil

moist   points   joined   choice

Garden Joy

Roy and Joy love to work in the garden. They enjoy digging and planting flowers. Roy waters every day to keep the soil moist. He points the hose at every plant. Roy and Joy joined the Garden Club. The Garden Club has a garden tour each year. If you buy a ticket you have a choice of gardens to visit. Roy and Joy have lots of visitors!

BLEND THE SOUNDS

DIPHTHONGS oi, oy /oi/: Use your finger to blend the sounds into a word. Draw a line to the picture that matches.

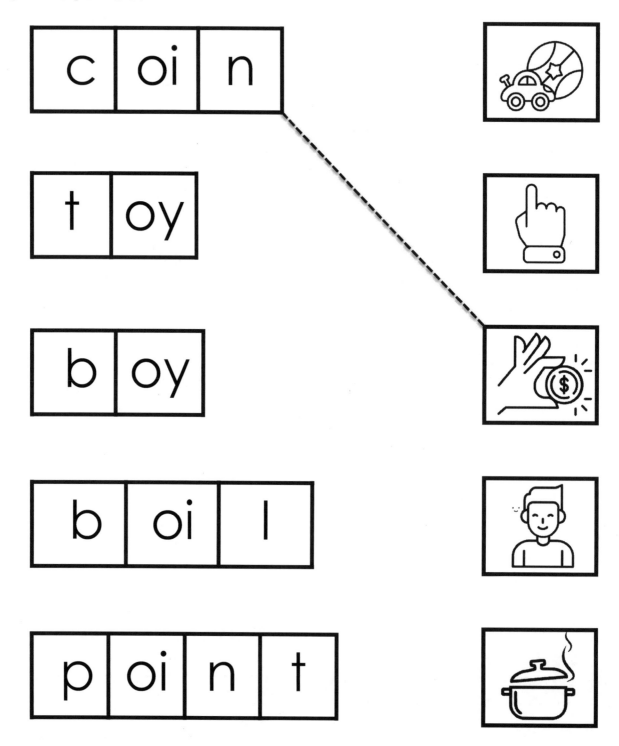

WRITE THE WORD

(93)

DIPHTHONGS oi, oy /oi/: Say the name of the picture. Sound it out. Find it in the word bank. Write the word on the line.

WORD BANK

| ☐ oyster | ☐ join | ☐ toy | ☐ coil | ☐ oil |

Word Sort

94

Diphthong: oy
Diphthong: oi

- ☐ toy
- ☐ join
- ☐ coy
- ☐ moist
- ☐ enjoy
- ☐ coin
- ☐ boy
- ☐ point
- ☐ soy
- ☐ spoil

Write the <u>oy</u> words here:

Write the <u>oi</u> words here:

Diphthongs: ou, ow /ow/

Point and Read: NEW WORDS

bounce	house	down	clown	loud
shout	howl	ground	crowd	around
bound				

Bounce House

Did you ever go to a bounce house? They are so much fun! You can jump up and down and act like a clown. Kids can be as loud as they want! Shout and howl as you bounce to the ground. You can even play games when you have a crowd. Bouncing balloons around is great too. If you go to a bounce house, you are bound to have fun!

BLEND THE SOUNDS

DIPHTHONGS ou, ow /ow/: Use your finger to blend the sounds into a word. Draw a line to the picture that matches.

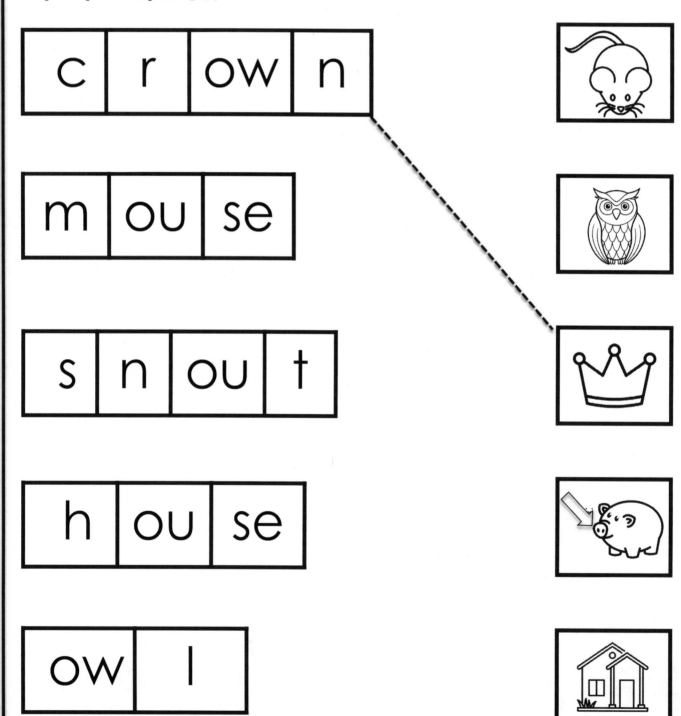

WRITE THE WORD

(97)

DIPHTHONGS ou, ow /ow/: Say the name of the picture. Sound it out. Find it in the word bank. Write the word on the line.

WORD BANK

| ☐ count | ☐ mouth | ☐ clown | ☐ cloud | ☐ cow |

Word Sort

98

Diphthong: ow
Diphthong: ou

☐ cow ☐ count ☐ owl ☐ shout ☐ howl
☐ house ☐ down ☐ round ☐ town ☐ found

Write the ow words here:

Write the ou words here:

Answer Key

pp. 12-14

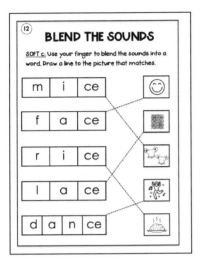
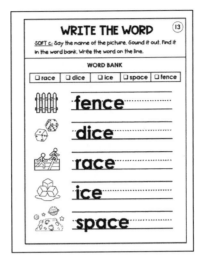
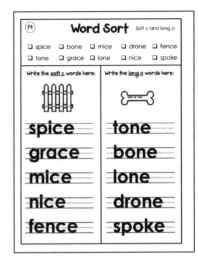

pp. 16-18

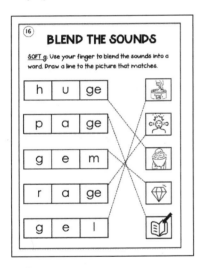

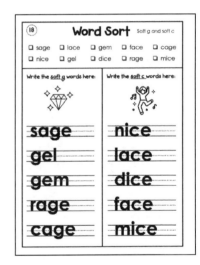

pp. 20-22

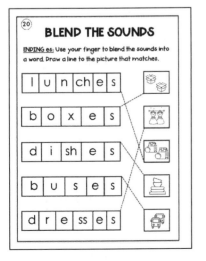
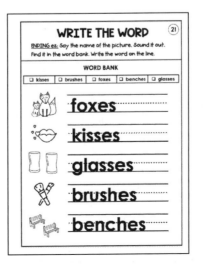
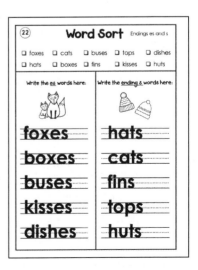

Answer Key

pp. 24-26

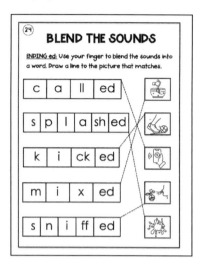

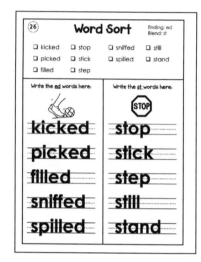

pp. 28-30

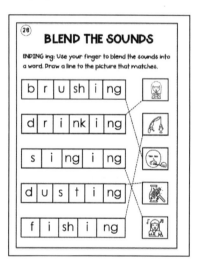

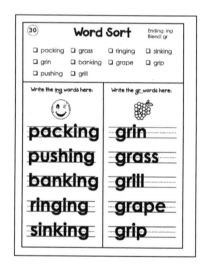

pp. 32-34

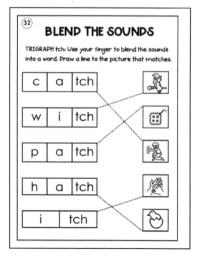
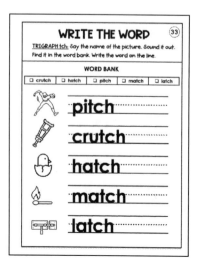

Answer Key

pp. 36-38

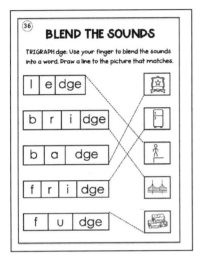
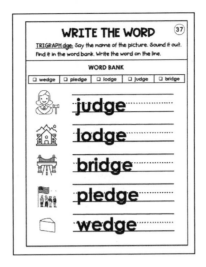
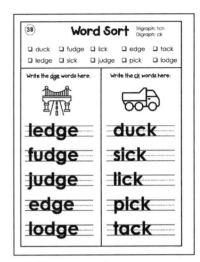

pp. 40-42

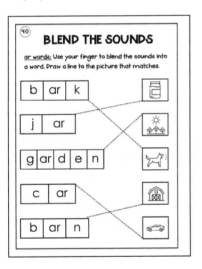
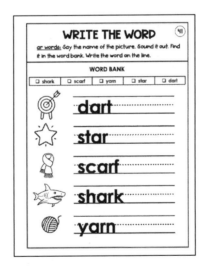
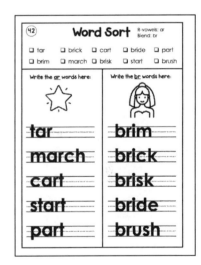

pp. 44-46

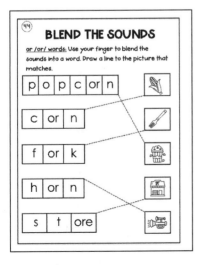

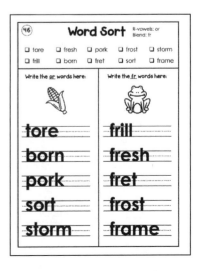

Answer Key

pp. 48-50

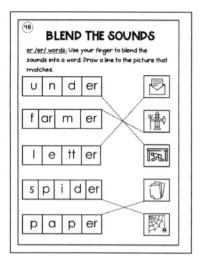 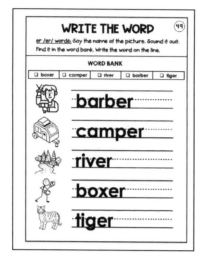 

pp. 52-54

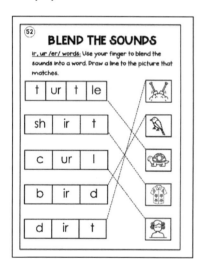  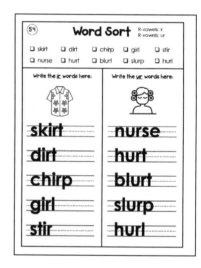

pp. 56-58

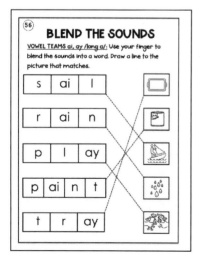  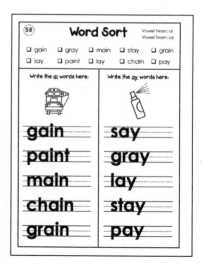

Answer Key

pp. 60-62

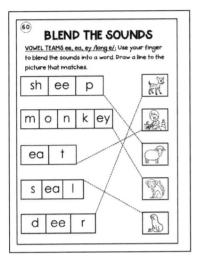
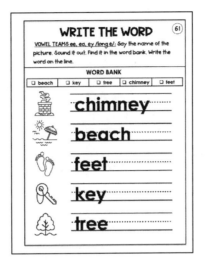
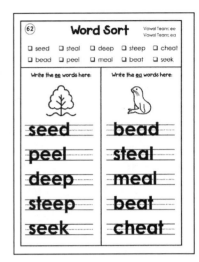

pp. 64-66

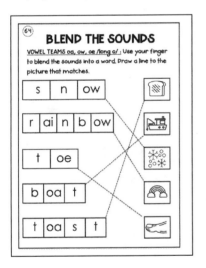
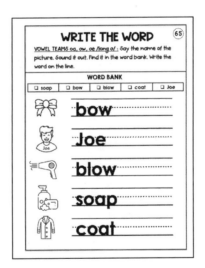
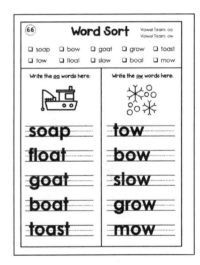

pp. 68-70

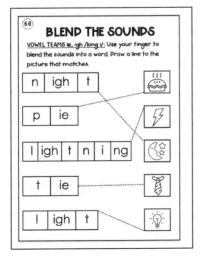

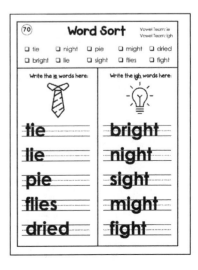

Answer Key

pp. 72-74

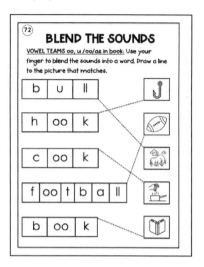

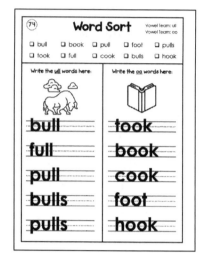

pp. 76-78

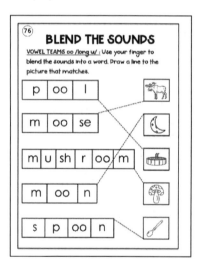

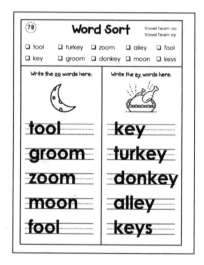

pp. 80-82

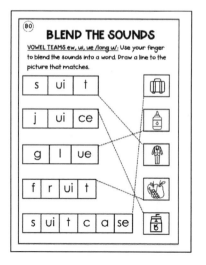
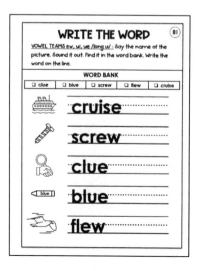
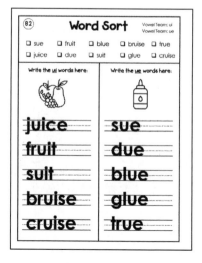

Answer Key

pp. 84-86

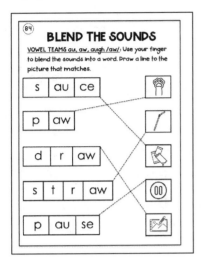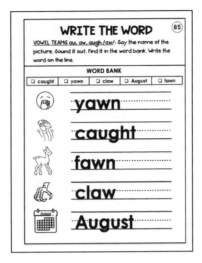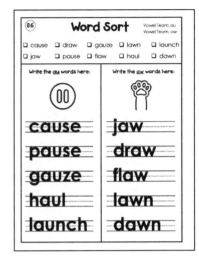

pp. 88-90

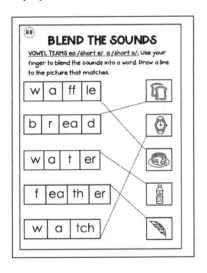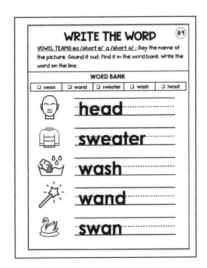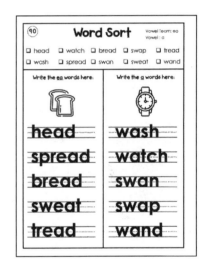

pp. 92-94

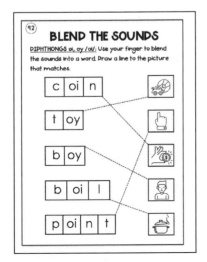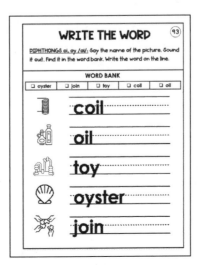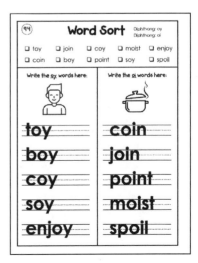

Answer Key

pp. 96-98

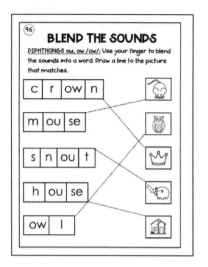

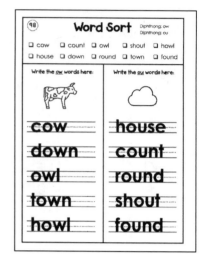

About the author:

Valerie Petrillo is an early childhood and special education educator. She is the author of several children's non-fiction books as well as educational products sold on TPT (Teachers Pay Teachers) and Amazon.

Visit Ladder to the Common Core for more educational products:

https://www.teacherspayteachers.com/Store/Ladder-to-the-Common Core

Visit the blog for lots of great teaching tips, strategies and freebies:

laddertothecommoncore.com

Made in the USA
Columbia, SC
11 April 2025